My Mother's Story

Polly Chapman

My Mother's Story

A Family Memory Book

Bedford Square
Publishers

Contents

Introduction   7

1. Early Life   9

2. Your Parents   23

3. Your School Days   37

4. Being a Teenager   51

5. Life After School   65

6. Your Friendships   75

7. Becoming a Mum   85

8. Being a Mum   97

9. Living Life Now   107

J. M. Barrie, *The Adventures of Peter Pan* (1911)

'It is the nightly custom of every good mother after her children are asleep to rummage in their minds and put things straight for the next morning.'

My Mother's Story

To my mother,

This journal is a way for me to find out more about you, to ask all the questions I forget to ask when we are living our everyday lives. There are the familiar stories I know about your past, the funny tales you have already shared, but there is so much I don't know and am eager to learn.

It's not just the big things – where you lived and where you went to school – that I want to know. I also want to hear about the small things, to build up a picture of how you lived before you became my mum. What music did you like? When did you first fall in love? And I'd like to know about the important stuff too, the challenges you faced and the life lessons you feel you can pass on to me.

Thank you for taking the time to do this. I'm excited to find out more about your past and to read your reflections on your life and on your experiences as my mum.

All mums have different journeys, so please ignore any questions that you feel are not relevant for you.

With all my love

....

George Eliot, *The Mill on the Floss* (1860)

'We could never have loved the earth so well if we had had no childhood in it.'

Early Life

In this section I'd love to hear all about your childhood. What are your earliest memories? What are the fragments that stay with you even if you can't remember events in a linear way? Maybe it's the wallpaper from your first bedroom, or a particular toy you treasured.

I'd also love to have a sense of the place where you were brought up – both the physical space of the house or flat you lived in, and the people around you who were important, or who particularly stick in your mind. I know it's not easy to dig that far back, but perhaps looking at photographs will help to prompt memories. And if you have any photographs you'd like to stick on the next page, that would be great!

These early years shaped the woman you are today, so please tell me as much as you can remember.

What are your earliest memories?

Where were you born? Can you describe the home in which you were raised?

What are your strongest memories of the area you were brought up in? Was there a particular park you were taken to? Or swimming pool? Was there a local shop you loved going to? Were you allowed to buy sweets when you were little?

_____

_____

_____

_____

_____

Did you have a garden? Can you describe it, and how you played in it?

_____

_____

_____

_____

_____

What are your earliest memories of your bedroom? Did you have any favourite toys? Did you share your bedroom?

Do you have any recollections of neighbours or babysitters from your early years? Who were the important people in your life other than your parents?

What do you remember about your early years of nursery and school? Can you remember your first day? Did you have a 'home corner' in your nursery? Are there special toys you remember playing with? Do you remember any teachers from nursery?

_____

_____

_____

_____

_____

_____

Are there any birthday parties or other celebrations that particularly stand out? Did you have party entertainers? What games did you play at birthday parties? Feel free to add photos here too!

_____

_____

_____

_____

_____

Were you a naughty child? Can you remember getting into trouble when you were little?

Were you close to your family? Do you have any photographs of you all together when you were small that you could stick in here?

Did you have any pets growing up? If so, what were they called? What did you do to help look after them? If you didn't have a pet, would you have wanted one?

Did you go on family holidays? Which were the ones you particularly remember?

Did you play games together as a family? What are the games you most enjoyed – are they the same as the ones we played?

What are the family gatherings or parties that you really remember from when you were growing up?

How often did you see your wider family – aunts, uncles, cousins? Are there relatives you saw a lot back then, but who you have lost touch with now?

What was your favourite food when you were little? Was the food you ate very different from the food you made for me? What is the one family recipe you would like pass on?

Fact File:

What was your first address?

How long did you live there?

What was the name of your favourite toy?

What was the name of your nursery school?

What was the name of your favourite babysitter?

Do you remember the name of your closest friend at nursery?

What was the name of your pet?

Christina Rossetti, *Sonnets Are Full of Love* (1881)

'I love you, Mother, I have woven a wreath
Of rhymes wherewith to crown your honoured name.'

Your Parents

I would love to know more about my grandparents here. I don't know much about their past, and since they are such an important part of your life, I feel I should hear some of your memories or stories about them.

It would be interesting to try and work out how much you followed the parenting style of your parents and the ways in which you tried to be different from them as a parent yourself. I know about them as my grandparents, but I'm sure they were different as parents! Were they strict? Were you close to them? What were their best qualities as parents? Think about the times you got into trouble or the moments when they were particularly proud of you.

I can see traits in myself that I have inherited from you: I'd like to know if there are personality traits you think you have inherited from your parents. What are the important ways in which you feel you were shaped by your upbringing?

Do you have any photographs of your mum you could stick here?

Tell me about your mum, what sort of person was she when you were growing up? Did she change as she got older?

_____

_____

_____

_____

_____

_____

Where had your mum been brought up, what sort of life had she lived?

_____

_____

_____

_____

_____

Did your mum work? If so, what did she do?

What sort of relationship did you have with her – were you close? Did your relationship with her change when you became a mum?

Are there any personality traits you think you inherited from your mum? Are there any interests you share with her? Do you enjoy any of the same activities or hobbies as her?

Were there any moments when you fell out with her?

Do you have any photographs of my grandfather that you could stick here?

Tell me about him, what sort of person was he?

Did he work? What did he do?

What was his background, and where had he been raised? Do you remember visiting his childhood home?

How close were you to him? Do you have memories of special times spent with him? Did he introduce you to things that you still enjoy?

_____
_____
_____
_____
_____
_____
_____

How did your parents meet?

_____
_____
_____
_____
_____
_____

Where did my grandparents live when you were born? Did they ever move?

_____

_____

_____

_____

_____

Do you think you are most like your mum or your dad? In what ways are you like them? Can you see any aspects of them in me?

_____

_____

_____

_____

_____

How do you think the way you were raised is different from the way you have raised me? Were there things about the way you were brought up that you wanted to make sure you did differently as a parent?

What were the best things you think your parents did for you?

Would you describe your childhood as happy? Is there anything you would change if you could?

Do you remember your own grandparents? What can you tell me about them?

Fact File
What were the full names of your mother and father?
What are their dates of birth?
What were the full names of your grandparents?
What are their dates of birth?
Where was your mother born?
Where was your father born?

Fact File
How many siblings did your mother have?
What are their names?
How many siblings did your father have?
What are their names?

Write three words for each of your parents that you think sum them up.

_____

_____

_____

_____

Your Parents

Frances Ellen Watkins Harper, *The Two Offers* (1859)

'Every mother should be a true artist, who knows how to weave into her child's life images of grace and beauty, the true poet capable of writing on the soul of childhood the harmony of love and truth, and teaching it how to produce the grandest of all poems – the poetry of a true and noble life.'

Your School Days

Please tell me everything you can about your school days. They are such formative years, and I'd be really interested to find out how you think they made you into the person you are today. It's probably easier to remember your secondary school, but if you can try and think back to primary school, I'd love to know what you remember as being good or bad, fun or boring. Was there a love of sport that started then? Or of art or reading? What are the overriding memories of your primary school days? I can remember a teacher I really didn't like and one who I really did – are there any teachers that stick in your mind?

I also wonder what you think were the most important aspects of your secondary school education. It might be a teacher who had a profound impact on your future career, or friends you made whilst you were there. Perhaps you first fell in love whilst at school or discovered a work ethic that has stayed with you since. I'd really like to know if your school days were happy or whether you would do anything differently if you could re-live them now.

Do you have a photograph of your first day at primary and/or secondary school that you can stick in here?

Where did you go to primary school? Can you remember anything about the buildings? Were you happy there?

_____
_____
_____
_____
_____

What are your strongest memories of primary school? Can you remember the names of any teachers who you loved, or ones who you really didn't like? Why did you love/dislike them?

_____
_____
_____
_____
_____
_____

Were there any talents that you developed at primary school that ended up becoming part of your life now?

Do you remember any of your friends from primary school? Are you still in touch with any of them?

Where did you go to secondary school? Did you enjoy your time there?

What was your favourite subject and why? Was it always your favourite or did you develop a love for it?

Did you have a favourite teacher? Was there someone who inspired you?

Were there subjects you really couldn't get on with? That you found baffling? What were your worst moments in class?

What are your favourite memories from school?

What were the most difficult times you had at school?

Were you into drama, art, sport or any other extracurricular activity? What did you enjoy most outside of regular lessons?

Were there any drama or dance productions, sports matches or school events that really stick in your mind?

Did you ever get into trouble? If so, what happened and what effect did it have on you? How did your parents react?

_____

_____

_____

_____

_____

_____

When you think about your school years, what lasting impact did they have on your character?

_____

_____

_____

_____

_____

_____

Was there a particular moment from your schooldays that stands out as being pivotal to your future life or career?

Can you find any old reports from school that you can photograph and stick in here? If not, do you remember what your reports said?

Fact File

What was the name of your secondary school?

What year did you start and when did you leave?

Who was your best friend at secondary school?

What exams did you take and what grades did you get?

What was your worst subject?

Describe your school uniform

What was the name of your headmaster or headmistress?

Fact File
What was your most embarrassing moment at school?
What was your proudest moment?
Were you a prefect or any other position of responsibility?

Sarojini Naidu, *Cradle Song* (1905)

*'Dear eyes, good night, In golden light
The stars around you gleam; On you I press
With soft caress
A little lovely dream.'*

Being a Teenager

Teenage years can be an emotional rollercoaster. It's a time when we figure out who we are and what we believe in. The highs and lows are intense and unforgettable, and some of my most vivid memories come from that time. It can be an exciting but also a confusing time of life and I'm keen to learn how you navigated it.

Do you think it was easier to be a teen when you were growing up than it was for me? I'm curious to know whether you had the same insecurities and anxieties as I did, or whether we shared any of the same dreams and goals. It's hard for me to imagine you as a teenager so please do share as much as you feel able to! I'd love to know about the memories that make you smile or to hear about the challenges you faced.

If you have any photographs, please stick them in here, I'd love to see photos of you with your friends or wearing outfits you loved at the time.

What sort of teenager were you? Did you ever fall out with your parents over things you wanted to do, but weren't allowed to?

Who was the person you most often turned to for advice when you were a teenager?

Can you remember your first kiss? Where did it happen, and how old were you?

Did you have a first love when you were at school? Who were they, and can you describe them?

Did you listen to a lot of music when you were at school? Who were your favourite bands or musicians?

How did you listen to them: radio, records, CDs? Did you make mixtapes?

Did you have a favourite book or film when you were a teenager?

Did you go to parties when you were a teenager? Did you enjoy them?

Was fashion important to you? Could you describe your style in a few words?

_____

_____

_____

_____

_____

Who were your best friends at the time? What did you all do together? Did you have a favourite place you would meet up?

_____

_____

_____

_____

_____

_____

Did you have part-time jobs whilst you were still at school? Do you remember how much you were paid?

What were the biggest news stories you remember?

What was the most embarrassing moment from those years?

Do you have any memories from that time that still make you laugh?

What were your dreams and aspirations? Did you know what you wanted to do for work? Where did you want to live?

What was the most challenging moment of your teenage years?

If there was one thing you could go back and change about that time, what would it be?

___

Fact File
Who was your first celebrity crush?
What was the first music concert you went to?
Where did you live when you were a teenager?

Fact File

What was the name of the pub or club where you most often met up with your friends?

How old were you when you went on holiday with friends for the first time?

Where did you go?

What was your favourite TV show?

How did you keep in touch with your friends before mobile phones?

Jane Austen, *Northanger Abbey* (1817)

*'A mother would have been always present.
A mother would have been a constant friend;
her influence would have been beyond all other.'*

Life After School

Did you know what you wanted to do when you left school? I would love to know more about the choices that you made at this stage, and how long it took you to work out the right path to follow. I wonder whether you found it all overwhelming, or whether you always knew what you wanted to do. Were your parents supportive at this stage, and happy with the decisions you were making? Did you listen to their advice or were you fixed on your own path?

I'm also interested in how you found the transition from school to the world of work or university. Did you enjoy the freedom, or were there challenges in navigating your way into adulthood? I wonder whether you look back now and are pleased with the choices you made, or whether there are things you wish you had done differently.

If you have any photographs of you at university or in the year when you left school, please stick them in here.

What did you do after leaving school? Had you got the grades you needed to move on to the next stage?

Did you go to university? Where did you go and what did you study? If not, did you go straight into work or an apprenticeship?

What were the best and worst things about university or your apprenticeship? Was there a particular moment that was a highlight?

Did you know what you wanted to do for a job or a career? How did you end up in your first job?

Where was your first job and what do you remember about your first day at work?

_____

_____

_____

_____

_____

_____

How quickly did you settle in and how long did you stay in your first job?

_____

_____

_____

_____

_____

_____

What did you most like about the work you were doing?

Did you make good friends at work? Who were they and are you still in touch with them?

What was the most embarrassing mistake you made while at work?

Was there an alternative career you wished you had pursued?

What is the most memorable experience of your working life?

Is there any advice you would give me on how to be successful and happy at work?

Fact File

Where was the first place you worked?

What was the name of your first boss?

How old were you when you got your first job?

What was your salary when you started work?

What is the most enjoyable job you have had?

What was the biggest mistake you made at work?

What was your greatest triumph at work?

Ann Taylor, *My Mother,* from Original Poems For Infant Minds (1804)

*'Who ran to help me when I fell,
And would some pretty story tell,
Or kiss the place to make it well?
My Mother.'*

Your Friendships

You've shown me through example the importance of friendship. You seem to have lots of friends, many of whom you have known for years. I'd like to know what qualities you look for in a friend, and the ways in which you have been a good friend to others.

I'm also interested to hear a little bit more about the ups and downs of friendship; what you've done when the path hasn't been smooth and how you've managed to patch things up. Do you have any tips to share?

I have lovely friends now, but were there moments in my past when you were worried about the friends I had? Were there ways you tried to steer me away from some people or did you think it better to leave me to find my own path?

Who were the first people you remember as being friends at school?

Did they stay as close friends? If not, why?

Do you remember a particularly significant falling out of friendship? What happened?

_____

_____

_____

_____

_____

_____

Did you succeed in making up with the friend after the bad falling out? If so, do you remember how you fixed it?

_____

_____

_____

_____

_____

_____

Were you part of one tightly bound friendship group at school or did you move between different groups?

What do you think drew you to those people?

What are the most important qualities you look for in a friendship? Has this changed over time?

_____

_____

_____

_____

_____

Can you give me an example when close friends have been there for you in difficult times?

_____

_____

_____

_____

_____

What does it take to be a good friend to others? Are there particular moments you look back on when you feel you were able to help a close friend?

What are the funniest, most joyous moments you have shared with friends?

Is there an ideal number of close friends to have?

What do you think of my friends? Were there any moments when you were worried about my friendships and, if so, what did you do about it?

How would your friends describe you?

Fact File

Who was your first friend?

Who has been your friend for the longest amount of time?

If you had to call a friend in an emergency, who would it be?

Fact File

Is there a friend who you really miss, but haven't seen in a long time?

Who is your best friend?

Do you have a favourite friend of mine?

Describe your friendship group with three words.

Elizabeth Gaskell, *Mary Barton* (1848)

'She saw her mother stand by her bedside, as she used to do "in the days of long ago"; with a shaded candle and an expression of ineffable tenderness, while she looked on her sleeping child.'

Becoming a Mum

This section will focus on how you felt about becoming a mum – it's such a huge life change, and understanding how you coped with it will help me to imagine you as a young woman, rather than just as my mum. I'm interested to find out what emotions you went through when you found out you were pregnant: were you happy, nervous or a combination of both? And I wonder how you felt whilst you were pregnant, whether it was an 'easy' pregnancy or if there were health challenges for you to deal with.

When I came along, how were the early stages of motherhood – did you have much help? Were your parents supportive? How did you cope with lack of sleep? I'm also really interested in how you adjusted to life as a young mother and what the hardest and the best moments were during those first few months. I'd be interested to know whether there was any advice or wisdom handed down from your parents, or whether you just had to figure it all out on your own.

If you have a photograph of you holding me just after I'd been born, please add it here.

When and how did you find out you were pregnant with me?

_____

_____

_____

_____

_____

_____

How did you feel while you were pregnant? Did you have any strange cravings? If you were working, how did you cope?

_____

_____

_____

_____

_____

_____

Did you take part in ante-natal groups? If so, did you make any good friends at this stage?

How was my birth? Can you tell me about the day I was born?

What were your first thoughts when you saw me? Did you know in advance whether I was going to be a boy or a girl?

Was the experience of giving birth what you expected? Who supported you during your labour?

What do you most remember from the early months of my life? Did you have much help from your friends or family?

What sort of baby was I? Needy? A good sleeper?

What did you most enjoy, and what were the worst bits about being the mother of a young child?

Was there a particular fashion in parenting when I was young? What was your philosophy in getting through those early years?

Did you read books or look for advice on how to be a good parent? Was there any good advice handed down from parents or in-laws?

What sacrifices did you have to make to become a mum? Was there anything about coping with motherhood at that point that you wish you had done differently?

Fact File

How old were you when you gave birth to me?

What was the name of the hospital where I was born?

How long were you in labour?

What time was I born?

How much did I weigh?

Fact File

How much time did you take off for maternity leave?

What was my first word?

How old was I when I took my first step?

Louisa May Alcott, *Little Women* (1868)

'The clocks were striking midnight and the rooms were very still as a figure glided quietly from bed to bed, smoothing a coverlid here, settling a pillow there, and pausing to look long and tenderly at each unconscious face, to kiss each with lips that mutely blessed, and to pray the fervent prayers which only mothers utter.'

Being a Mum

It can't be easy being a mum, but you are brilliant at it. I'd really like to know how it feels for you, emotionally, to be a mother. You are always there for me, but how do you manage to be so caring and always show up for all of us, no matter what? I want to believe it's a superpower bestowed on you when you become a mum, but I know that's not the case!

This is where I pick your brains about the lessons you've learnt as a mother, about the highs and lows, and how becoming a mother has changed the person you've become. Of course, I'd also love to know when you have been proudest of me and when you've been most fed up!

Can you stick a photograph of the two of us together here?

How do you think becoming a mother changed you as a person?

What is the hardest thing about being a mum?

What are the funniest moments you remember from when I was growing up?

What was the scariest thing that happened when I was a child?

Are there family traditions we have that you carried on from when you were young? Why do you think these traditions are important?

Were there moments when you were particularly proud of me?

Were there times when you were particularly worried about me or exasperated with me?

Is there anything you feel you got wrong as a mother? Anything you would change if you were to do it all again?

What did you think of my first romantic partner?

What tips would you give to someone who is hoping to combine parenthood with having a career?

What top tips would you give to someone who is about to become a mum?

_____

_____

_____

_____

_____

_____

Fact File
What was the worst illness I had as a child?
What was my favourite food when I was little?
Where was our best family holiday from your point of view?

Fact File

What was my naughtiest moment?

What was my first word?

Can you describe my personality as a child in three words?

What was my favourite toy?

Was I a quiet or talkative child?

Was I a picky eater or adventurous with food?

If you could re-live one day of my childhood, which would it be?

Beatrix Potter, *The Tale of Peter Rabbit* (1901)

'"Now, my dears," said old Mrs Rabbit one morning, "you may go into the fields or down the lane, but don't go into Mr McGregor's garden..."'

Living Life Now

Being a mother is only one part of your identity, and I'd like to know how you feel as you look back over the past and look forward to the next stage of your life. This chapter is where I can find out how you view your own history, and what your dreams are for the future.

I'm also really interested to find out what you think the most significant changes have been over your lifetime, and what you think the world will look like in another fifty years. What do you think there is to look forward to or to be afraid of?

But it's not just the serious stuff – I'd also like to know about the everyday things – what is your perfect way to spend a Sunday? What is your favourite ice-cream flavour and what is your desert island meal?

And finally, I want to know the one piece of advice you'd like to pass on as a result of all your life experience.

Thank you, Mum!

What is the hardest decision you've ever had to make? Would you make it again?

Is there anything you've done that you regret and would do differently now?

Is there anything you haven't told me about in your life that you can share now for the first time?

What are the most significant world events that have happened in your lifetime?

What are the greatest changes, technological and social, that you have seen in your life so far?

___

What do you think I have to look forward to, but also that you worry about in the future?

___

What are your own dreams for the future? What do you want to do next?

_____

_____

_____

_____

_____

_____

What makes you happy or brings you the most joy?

_____

_____

_____

_____

_____

_____

Can you describe your perfect day?

If there was a particular day in your life that you could go back and re-live, which one would it be?

What is on your bucket list?

_____

_____

_____

_____

_____

_____

_____

If you could re-live your life are there any important decisions you would change? If so, what are they?

_____

_____

_____

_____

_____

_____

_____

Please can you share your three favourite recipes with me here.

___

What are the most important practical skills you think I should learn?

Which countries are the ones you would most like to visit in the future?

_____

_____

_____

_____

_____

Is there something new you feel you would like to achieve in your life?

_____

_____

_____

_____

_____

_____

Are there any adventures you would like to go on with me?

What are your hopes for me for the future?

What are you most grateful for?

What do you think was the best thing you did for us as a mother?

What is the advice you would most like me to take forward in my life?

___

Fact File
What is your date of birth?
What is your height?
What is your favourite ice-cream flavour?

Fact File

What is your desert island meal?

What are your top three desert island discs?

What animal would you be?

What is your favourite colour

Where would you live if you could live anywhere?

Milk chocolate or dark chocolate?

Town or country?

Ralph Waldo Emerson, *Journal* (1836)

'There never was a child so lovely but his mother was glad to get asleep.'

Can you sketch out a Family Tree here? Go as far back as you can!

These last few pages are a space for you to add anything you'd like to say to me that hasn't been covered in this journal. Please do also add any sketches, photographs or poems that are fun or meaningful to you. Do you have any of the early stories or poems you might have written? Or perhaps there are some of mine from when I was young that you have kept and could reproduce here?

First published in the UK in 2026 by Bedford Square Publishers Ltd,
London, UK

bedfordsquarepublishers.co.uk
@bedsqpublishers

© Polly Chapman, 2026

The right of Polly Chapman to be identified as the author of this work has been asserted in accordance with the Copyright, Designs and Patents Act 1988. All rights reserved. No part of this book may be reproduced, stored in or introduced into a retrieval system, or transmitted, in any form or by any means (electronic, mechanical, photocopying, recording or otherwise) without the written permission of the publishers.

Any person who does any unauthorised act in relation to this publication may be liable to criminal prosecution and civil claims for damages.
A CIP catalogue record for this book is available from the British Library.

ISBN
978-1-83501-537-7 (Hardback)

2 4 6 8 10 9 7 5 3 1

Typeset in Larken by Palimpsest Book Production Ltd, Falkirk, Stirlingshire

Printed in Great Britain by CPI Group (UK) Ltd, Croydon CR0 4YY

The manufacturer's authorised representative in the EU for product safety is Easy Access System Europe,
Mustamäe tee 50, 10621 Tallinn, Estonia
gpsr.requests@easproject.com